ZOO ANIMALS
IN THE WILD

ELEPHANT

JINNY JOHNSON

ILLUSTRATED BY GRAHAM ROSEWARNE

A+

Smart Apple Media

Published by Smart Apple Media
2140 Howard Drive West, North Mankato, Minnesota 56003

Designed by Helen James
Illustrated by Graham Rosewarne

Photographs by Robert E. Barber, Corbis (Tony Arruza, Sharna Balfour; Gallo Images,
Alissa Crandall, Nigel J. Dennis; Gallo Images, Nicole Duplaix, D. Robert & Lorri Franz,
Gallo Images, Roger De La Harpe; Gallo Images, Martin Harvey, Eric and David
Hosking, Peter Johnson, Stephanie Maze, Jim McDonald, Joe McDonald, Charles O'Rear,
Ron Sachs, RADU SIGHETI/Reuters, Paul A. Souders), Wildlife Conservation Society
(B. Meng, D. Shapiro)

Printed and bound in Thailand

Library of Congress Cataloging-in-Publication Data

Johnson, Jinny.
Elephant / by Jinny Johnson.
p. cm. — (Zoo animals in the wild)
Includes index.
ISBN 1-58340-643-3
1. Elephants—Juvenile literature. I. Title.

QL737.P98J617 2005
599.67—dc22   2004059199

First Edition

9 8 7 6 5 4 3 2 1

Contents

Elephants

Elephants are gentle giants. They are the biggest of all land animals, but they can walk along making barely a sound on their broad, padded feet. Elephants are strong enough to pull up whole trees but will softly stroke a newborn calf.

An elephant has a huge, bulky body, a big head, and large, floppy ears. Its legs are like thick pillars, strong enough to carry the animal's heavy body.

A family of African elephants.

More than 1,000 elephants live in zoos all over the world. They are among the most popular of all zoo animals.

There is a scattering of hair on its thick, wrinkly skin and a little tuft of hair at the end of its tail. An elephant also has a long nose called a trunk, and some elephants have long, pointed tusks. Male elephants are much bigger than female elephants.

The thick pads on an elephant's foot muffle the sound of anything it steps on.

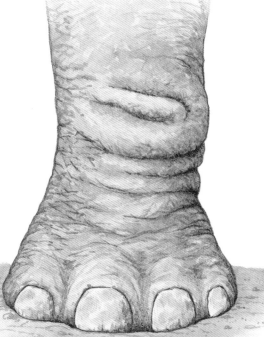

5

Elephant tusks

Tusks are actually big teeth. Baby elephants are born with little tusks, but these fall out after a few months.
Young elephants grow new tusks when they are about a year old. The tusks keep growing throughout an elephant's life.

Tusks are amazingly useful. An elephant uses its tusks to dig up plants to eat, strip bark and break branches off trees, or lift

Elephants often use one tusk more than the other.

Zoo elephants are given branches so they can strip off the bark with their tusks just like they do in the wild. Sometimes tusks get chipped or broken. Zoo elephants are lucky—if a tusk is damaged, they get a visit from the zoo dentist, who repairs it.

fallen trees out of the way. Tusks also make good weapons when male elephants decide to fight each other.

Male elephants sometimes fight over females.

An elephant's trunk

The most unusual thing about an elephant is its long trunk. An elephant's trunk is made up of its nose and upper lip. Its nostrils are at the end of its trunk.

An elephant drinks by sucking up water with its trunk, then squirting it into its mouth.

An elephant can eat, drink, and smell with its trunk. It can also pick things up. The trunk is strong, but it's also very sensitive. An elephant uses its trunk to stroke a baby elephant or to pat a friend to say hello.

A loving mother strokes her baby with her long trunk.

Sometimes an elephant picks up sticks or twigs with its trunk and uses them to scratch itself or get rid of an annoying insect.

An elephant gathers leaves with its trunk and stuffs them into its mouth.

African and Asian elephants

There are two kinds of elephants—African elephants and Asian elephants. African elephants are bigger than Asian elephants and have larger ears. The African elephant's back dips slightly in the middle, while the Asian elephant has a high, rounded back.

Both male and female African elephants have long tusks, but the male's tusks are usually longer than the female's. Most male Asian elephants have tusks, but they are smaller than those of African elephants. Female Asian elephants don't have tusks.

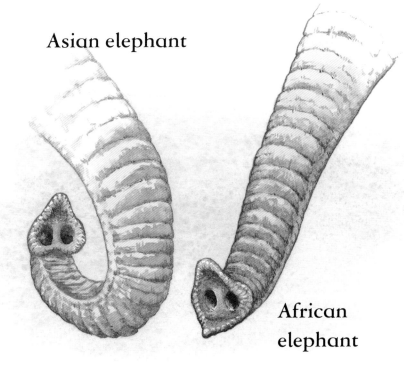

Asian elephant

African elephant

There are both African elephants and Asian elephants living in zoos. Zookeepers take care of both in the same way.

An Asian elephant in a zoo (above) and an African elephant in the wild (right).

At the end of the African elephant's trunk are two little "fingers" that help it grab things. The Asian elephant has only one finger at the end of its trunk.

At home in the wild

Wild elephants live in places where there are plenty of plants to eat and lots of fresh water to drink. They also like to be near trees, which can shelter them from the hot sun. When they get hot, elephants cool off by flapping their big ears.

At midday, when the sun is very hot, elephants like to rest under a shady tree.

Big ears help elephants get rid of extra heat.

Elephants gather to take a refreshing drink.

Because elephants eat so much, they need to move around a lot to find enough food. Most spend several hours a day walking.

Elephants don't have many enemies—they're too big for most creatures to attack. But mothers do have to keep baby elephants safe from big cats such as lions and tigers.

At home in the zoo

It is difficult to keep large animals such as elephants in zoos. Elephants need a lot of space and the company of other elephants. The best zoos keep groups of elephants in areas big enough for them to wander around.

Elephants need a large, grassy area to move around in, as well as shelters where they can hide from view when they want to. They also need fresh water or

A zookeeper weighs an elephant as part of its regular health check.

Elephants are good swimmers. They swim underwater using their trunk like a snorkel.

mud to roll in and scratching posts to rub against. Elephant enclosures used to have concrete floors, which were hard on the animals' feet, but newer elephant homes have sand floors.

Family life

Elephants are friendly animals, and they like the company of other elephants. Female elephants live in family groups. The family may include a great-grandmother, grandmother, and aunts, as well as young.

The family is led by the oldest female, who decides where they will go and what they will do each day.

Elephants in a family stay close together as they move from place to place.

All of the elephants in the family help take care of the babies. Male elephants leave their mother's family when they are about 12 years old. They join herds of other males or live alone.

An elephant says hello by touching another elephant's head and mouth with its trunk.

Most zoos don't have enough space to keep a big elephant family. Young elephants born in a zoo usually have to leave their mother sooner than they would in the wild.

Elephant babies

A female elephant gives birth to her first baby, called a calf, when she's between 10 and 20 years old. She carries her baby for a very long time before it's born—usually about 22 months but sometimes as long as 25 months.

The newborn calf struggles to its feet about half an hour after birth and has its first drink of milk shortly afterwards.

Other elephants in a family nudge a newborn calf with their trunks to help it stand up.

A newborn baby elephant weighs twice as much as a full-grown man.

A calf stays close to its mother and other members of the family for safety.

Even though the calf manages to stand so quickly, it's a couple of days before it is strong enough to move with the herd. All of the other elephants get excited when a calf is born and gather around to greet the new arrival.

Growing up

A baby elephant has a lot to learn. At first, it's not sure what to do with its trunk and has to learn how to use it for drinking, eating, and many other things. The calf's mother and the other adult elephants in the family teach the youngster what to eat and how to find water.

A young elephant drinks its mother's milk until it is four years old or older. But it starts to eat some plants, too, when it is about six months old.

By the time a young female is about four years old, she'll spend a lot of her time helping to look after younger elephants in the family. But a male of that age starts to spend more time away from the family, playing with other young males.

Two young elephants nuzzle and play together.

Zoo elephants need toys so they don't get bored. Some elephants like to kick a ball around—especially if it's filled with tasty treats such as raisins or nuts.

An elephant's day

An elephant spends as much as three-quarters of its time looking for food and eating. It moves around during the morning and evening and at night but usually takes it easy for a while around midday.

In the evening, an elephant family often goes to a water hole to drink and bathe. The elephants spray themselves and each other with water and may roll over in the mud until their bodies are covered.

An elephant often sleeps standing up, leaning against a tree or another elephant.

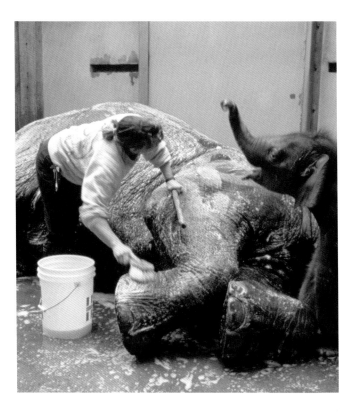

Zookeepers help elephants stay clean. They wash the elephants every day and scrub them with wire brushes to remove dirt and dead skin. They check their feet, too, to make sure there are no stones or sharp twigs stuck in the soft pads.

A layer of mud helps protect an elephant's skin from sunburn and biting insects.

Baby elephants enjoy a roll in the mud.

Big eaters

Elephants eat huge amounts of grass, leaves, twigs, and roots. An elephant can strip leaves from a branch with its trunk or dig up roots with its tusks. If an elephant wants to reach fresh green leaves at the top of a tree, it may just push the tree over.

A full-grown male elephant eats about 310 pounds (140 kg) of food a day. That would be like eating

Elephants strip bark from trees and eat it.

150 heads of lettuce, 300 apples, and 200 potatoes! An elephant also drinks a lot of water—at least two bathtubs' worth every day.

An elephant can suck as much as two gallons (8 l) of water into its trunk at one time.

Elephants in the zoo are given plenty of grass and hay to eat, and sometimes they get special treats such as carrots, apples, and watermelon, too. Food is sometimes hidden so the elephants have to search for it.

Keeping in touch

Elephants in a family are very friendly and like to talk to each other. Elephants make many different noises, from loud trumpeting calls to as many as 20 different deep rumbling sounds, some of which humans can't hear.

When elephants meet, they say hello with a low rumble that sounds like a loud purr. If a baby is frightened or lost, it makes loud bellowing sounds. Elephants can hear each other's calls from a long distance away. They also have very sensitive feet and can feel the ground vibrate from the calls of elephants that are far away.

An elephant raises its trunk as it calls.

Elephants send messages to each other with a wide range of movements and sounds.

Elephants also show their feelings with their ears. An elephant may flap its ears to show it's excited or happy—such as when a baby is born.

Zoo elephants get to know their keepers well. They will **sometimes** greet them with rumbling calls and flapping ears.

Elephant fact file

Here is some more information about elephants. Your mom and dad might like to read this so you can talk about elephants some more when you see them at the zoo, or perhaps you can read these pages together.

Elephants

An elephant is a mammal. There are two different species, or kinds, of elephants—African elephants and Asian elephants. All elephants eat plants.

Where elephants live

African elephants live in parts of Africa south of the Sahara. Asian elephants live in India, Sri Lanka, and parts of Southeast Asia.

Elephant numbers

Experts think there are probably about 500,000 elephants in Africa and about 35,000 in Asia. This might sound like a lot, but it is far fewer than there were 20 years ago. Elephants have suffered because poachers kill them for their tusks and because some of the areas where they live have been destroyed.

Size

A male African elephant stands about 13 feet (4 m) tall, weighs 13,000 pounds (6,000 kg), and has tusks that weigh up to 110 pounds (50 kg) each. A female African elephant stands up to 9 feet (2.7 m) tall, weighs 6,000 pounds (2,800 kg), and has tusks that weigh up to 15 pounds (7 kg) each.

A male Asian elephant stands about 10 feet (3 m) tall, weighs about 12,000 pounds (5,500 kg), and has tusks that weigh about 40 pounds (18 kg) each. A female Asian elephant stands about 8 feet (2.5 m) tall and weighs about 5,500 pounds (2,500 kg). Female Asian elephants do not have tusks.

Find out more

If you want to learn more about elephants, check out these Web sites:

Born Free Elefriends Campaign
www.bornfree.org.uk/elefriends

World Wildlife Fund: Elephants
 www.worldwildlife.org/elephants

Save the Elephants
www.save-the-elephants.org

Glossary

Bark
The outer covering of a tree trunk.

Calf
A young animal such as
an elephant.

Enclosure
The area where an animal
lives in a zoo.

Herd
A group of animals
such as elephants.

Mammal
A warm-blooded animal, usually with four legs and at
least some hair on its body. Female mammals feed their
babies with milk from their own body.

Poacher
Someone who hunts an animal illegally.

Strip
To pull off.

Vibrate
Move quickly back and forth.

Water hole
A pool or a dip in the ground where water collects and animals can drink.

Index